Look at Our Coins

by Gloria Chen

I have coins in my bank. I can find out how much money I have.

Let's see how I can use my money.

A penny is worth 1¢.
There are 8 pennies
in my bank. I have 8¢.

penny

1¢

Look at these toys.
Which toy can I buy?

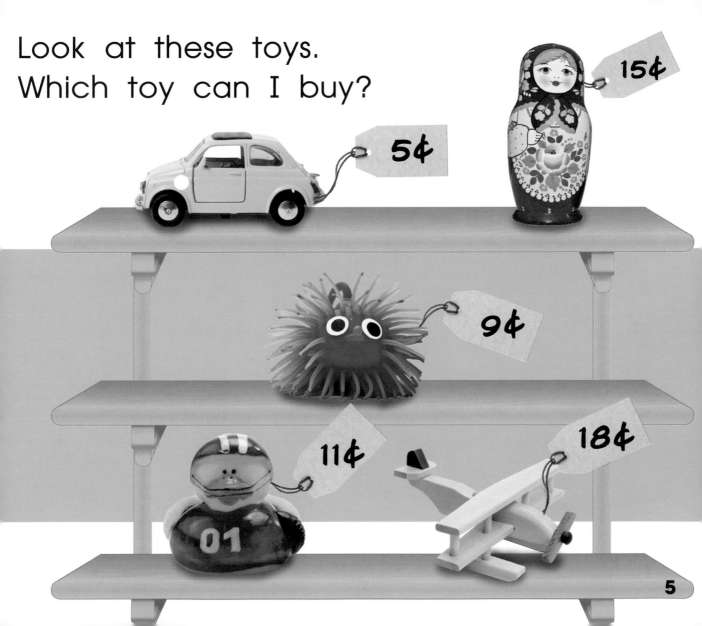

15¢

5¢

9¢

11¢

18¢

01

I have 7 nickels in my bank. A nickel is worth 5¢.

nickel

5¢

I have 35¢ in nickels.
What can I buy with 35¢?

55¢

70¢

25¢

40¢

60¢

I have some dimes in my bank, too. There are 6 dimes. A dime is worth 10¢.

dime

10¢

My brother counts by tens to find out how much money I have in dimes. I have 60¢ in dimes.

10, 20, 30, 40, 50, 60

9

A quarter is worth
more than a dime.
A quarter is worth 25¢.

quarter

25¢

I have 50¢ in quarters. A glass of lemonade is 75¢. Can I buy a glass of lemonade?

A nickel is worth 5¢, so 5 pennies are equal to 1 nickel.

1¢   1¢   1¢   1¢   1¢   5¢

I know a dime is worth 10¢.
I know that 2 nickels have
the same value as 1 dime.

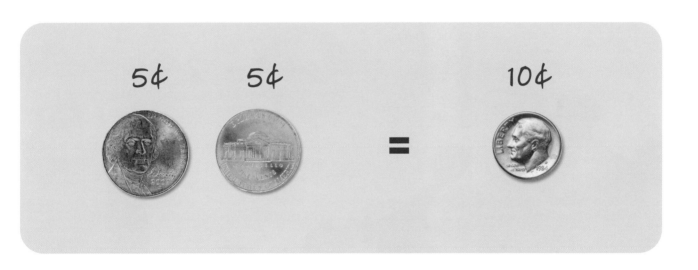

5¢   5¢   10¢

=

5¢   10¢

I can use coins from my bank
to go on this ride. I need 25¢.
I could use a quarter.

TICKET 891846   = 25¢

I could use 25 pennies. I could use 5 nickels, too. What other ways could I make 25¢?

= 25¢

= 25¢

I have pennies and nickels.
I have dimes and quarters.
I put my coins back in
my bank.